Neural Networks

*A Practical Guide for
Understanding and Programming
Neural Networks and Useful
Insights for Inspiring Reinvention*

Steven Cooper

creating a secondary or tertiary copy of the work or a recorded copy and is only allowed with an express written consent from the Publisher. All additional right reserved.

The information in the following pages is broadly considered to be a truthful and accurate account of facts, and as such any inattention, use or misuse of the information in question by the reader will render any resulting actions solely under their purview. There are no scenarios in which the publisher or the original author of this work can be in any fashion deemed liable for any hardship or damages that may befall them after undertaking information described herein.

Additionally, the information in the following pages is intended only for informational purposes and should thus be thought of as universal. As befitting its nature, it is presented without assurance regarding its prolonged validity or interim quality. Trademarks that are mentioned are done without written consent and can in no way be considered an endorsement from the trademark holder.

Table of Contents

Preface

The main purpose of this book is to provide the reader with the most elementary knowledge of neural networks fundamentals so that they can understand what these are all about.

Book Objectives

This book will help you:

- ✓ Know more about the fundamental principles of neural networks and how to understand and program neural networks in more detail.

- ✓ Have an elementary grasp of neural network concepts and tools that will make this work easier to do.

- ✓ Have achieved a technical background in neural networks and deep learning and appreciate its power.

Target Users

The book is designed for a variety of target audiences. The most suitable users would include:

- Newbies in computer science techniques and deep learning

- Professionals in neural networks and deep learning

- Professors, lecturers or tutors who are looking to find better ways to explain the content to their students in the simplest and easiest way

- Students and academicians, especially those focusing on neural networks and deep learning

Is this book for me?

This book is for those who are interested in neural networks and deep learning. There are a lot of skills that a data scientist needs, such as coding, intellectual mindset, eagerness to make new discoveries, and much more.

It's important that you are interested in this because you are obsessed with this kind of work. Little programming experience is required. If you already wrote a few lines of code and recognize basic programming statements, then this book is for you.

Introduction

"Despite how it's portrayed in books and movies, artificial intelligence is not a synthetic brain floating in a case of blue liquid somewhere. It is an algorithm -- a mathematical equation that tells a computer what functions to perform... In the world of AI, the Holy Grail is to discover the single algorithm that will allow machines to understand the world -- the digital equivalent of the Standard Model that lets physicists explain the operations of the universe." - **Jeff Goodell**

The multiplication of complex mathematical matrices is an idea that may have your eyelids feeling heavy already. It's quite common to see no practical use for performing such an abstract function. Even with the assistance of a computer, what purpose could be combining these arbitrary data sets serve?

It was discovered that we could define a computer program capable of a superficial, simulated version of learning. The key difference in nature between this new style of programming versus its predecessor is that conventional computer programs contained specific rules and operations to be performed upon execution of the program. Once the program was coded by its engineer(s), the code was locked into place until an update or software patch was released. The advent of computer code possessing the capacity to "learn" marked a new category of software in which a developer could write an initial function, though, over time, the function would correct, optimize, and rewrite itself. We call these types of software as neural networks, and their special ability is called machine learning.

Have you noticed the increasing prevalence of software that tries to learn from you? More and more, we are interacting with machines and platforms that try to predict what we are looking for. From movie and television show recommendations on Netflix based on your taste to the keyboard on your smartphone trying to predict and recommend the next word you may want to type, it's becoming obvious that machine learning will definitely be part of our future.

You have selected a wonderful time to get involved engaging and improving this amazing technology. Historically, this field has seen its growth in spurts. It is safe to say that, from here, neural networks should continue to experience steady growth. While that is an exciting news, this book will challenge you to accelerate the progress of neural networks and machine learning. We will discover what they can do and what they cannot do.

Don't be mystified. This is not magic, and it's hardly intelligence. The men and women that create and shape this concept of computer thinking have tremendous intelligence in comparison to the function they've created. And relative to them, you certainly possess only a bit more or less intellect. What I'm saying is that we are all above this concept.

Do you remember back in school when your math teacher taught your class about a matrix or matrices? A matrix is basically this series of numbers, sometimes positive, sometimes negative. The numbers are arranged to align to an invisible grid, separated by commas, and the entire grid of numbers is wrapped in fitting brackets. A matrix can have many different dimensional configurations (sizes). It can have the dimensionality of a skinny vertical rectangle or a square or a skinny horizontal rectangle, and everything in between. They feature these various configurations due to the types of data the particular matrix is holding. Having the flexibility to be used for many purposes is the influence of shape and size. Matrices can be added, subtracted, multiplied, and divided with others. Maybe it is easy and fun for you to work with sets of data in this way or maybe all you can remember clearly about matrices is that you hated them. Neural networks will give you a chance to experience them visually and subsequently, realize their practicality and potential.

This book won't go much into the mathematical side of a neural network, but you need to know how they relate to a matrix in order to be sufficiently oriented with the subject. This will be covered later in the book, but before we proceed, the previous sentence contains a major point worth emphasizing.

There is a logical, theoretical, and mathematical way of looking at a neural network. The second way is to approach it from an operational, functional, and creative standpoint. At the end of the day, it's true that a neural network is just a sophisticated math problem. Understanding them from a mathematical side lends an engineer great insights on how to affect change to a network since it is mathematical in nature. Their perspective enables them to enhance the efficiency of the technology that already exists. This is their strength. Their work has refined networks to perform in the practical ways that they do for us today. Strength in this domain should always try to be balanced equally with our second approach, however. Having the intellectual capacity to comprehend the operational nature in which a network performs should not be underestimated. Understanding the principles of what is at work will heighten your intuition for how it should be practiced. Being able to relate these functions to the nature in which we function will uncover breakthroughs that are hiding in plain sight. Those with this perspective in the field go forth proposing new models, transforming the field of machine learning. Regardless of which group you belong to, this book will enhance your understanding regarding the perspective centered on the operational and creative principles of neural network technology.

One thing we can say for sure is that they are useful for classifying or clustering data. Data classification is a task we can have a neural network perform that involves properly identifying certain types of inputs. Responses from these types of networks represent only its best guess. Ideally, the network becomes better over time at properly identifying or classifying these inputs through the process of regression.

Data clustering is an operation that involves pattern recognition between data sets. These networks help to show what's common among data that may have no clear structure. Data clustering is used in networks that analyze statistical data or analyze data in order to make predictions.

In the following pages, you will learn the history of neural networks and the way modern neural networks function. This book will share some emerging projects in the industry. Also, there will be some salient points offered about how to improve what we're working with today, rather than waiting for the advancement of the hardware hosting neural net technology. You will learn an effective technique for hacking into a neural network, supplemented by a countermeasure that will safeguard against this type of attack while simultaneously getting the ball rolling in the reader's mind for the proper treatment of other network vulnerabilities. Some "starter code" using the Python programming language will be provided, along with some introductory advice for modifying parameters in the code-based environment. Most of all, this book will feed the abstract reasoning region of your mind so that you are able to theorize and invent new types and styles of machine learning. You will see that there is a vast room for improvement.

Neural Networks

Origin

"Whatever you are studying right now, if you are not getting up to speed on deep learning, neural networks, etc., you lose. We are going through the process where software will automate software, automation will automate automation." - **Mark Cuban**

The point here is not to bore you with details that are less than practical. There are, however, some key points from the history of neural networks that are worth sharing to help enhance your perspective as sometimes understanding the history of a thing is the best way to understand how it works and where its technology is likely to progress in the future. You will learn which components of neural networks are newest to the field versus foundational aspects. There is also something to appreciate about the efforts, trial-and-error, and multiple revivals on the subject.

Neural networks are nearly as old as computers themselves, thought they have only started to become mainstream relatively recently. The reason for this is that they have not been seen as stable progress as computers have, as their progress is often gated by issues that take years, if not decades, to fix. In recent years, interest in neural networks has reached an all-time high. We now have networks that can recognize speech, classify subjects in a photo or video, and much more! You will see that their evolution is fascinating.

1940s

Neurophysiologist Warren McCulloch and Walter Pitts, a mathematician, detailed how neurons work in a paper written in 1943. They also produced a demonstration of how a simple neural network functioned using electrical circuits.

Later, in 1949 Donald Hebb authored *The Organization of Behavior,* where he introduced that neural pathways were strengthened each time they were used. Neurons firing together in the brain reinforced and improved their connections. This is an integral part of how the human brain learns and refines information.

1950s

With the advancement of computer processors in the 1950s, it became possible to engineer an artificial neural network that operated in much the same way as the human brain. Leading this initiative at the time was IBM researcher Nathanial Rochester. He was unsuccessful in achieving this in his first attempt, however. In 1955, IBM mathematician John McCarthy and Marvin Minsky proposed to Rochester to host a conference on the topic of machine intelligence.

After receiving seven thousand dollars in funding from the Rockefeller Foundation, a conference that has since been considered "the birth of artificial intelligence," was held in the summer of 1956, quite possibly changing the world forever in the process.

"We propose that a 2 month, 10-man study of artificial intelligence be carried out during the summer of 1956 at Dartmouth College in Hanover, New Hampshire.

The study is to proceed on the basis of the conjecture that every aspect of learning or any other feature of intelligence can in principle be so precisely described that a machine can be made to simulate it. An attempt will be made to find how to make machines use language, form abstractions and concepts, solve kinds of problems now reserved for humans, and improve themselves." - Dartmouth AI Project Proposal; J. McCarthy et al.; Aug. 31, 1955.

The Dartmouth AI conference is practically the 'ground zero' of the AI field as virtually all research in the field can be traced back to this point. This conference revealed the most relevant information known at the time, along with some thought-provoking ideas about what the future of artificial intelligence could bring. Many advanced researchers were invited. Some of the attending guests were researching fields such as:

- Complexity theory

- Language simulation

- Neuron nets

- Abstraction

- Effects of randomness on creative thinking

This event is especially emphasized in this timeline, as it was the largest gathering regarding machine learning and AI in history to that point, and would remain the largest gathering of likeminded individuals in the field for decades to come. The conference also stirred up controversy over the possibility that given the advancement of technology at that time, soon the world would be facing a scenario where machines were as intelligent as humans. Their question was the same as ours today – "when?"

By 1959, two men Bernard Widrow and Marcian Hoff developed a model ADALINE and MADALINE. These names stood for (Multiple) Adaptive Linear Elements. ADALINE could recognize binary patterns, and MADALINE was the first neural network to be used in real-world applications.

1960s & 70s

In the early 1960s, despite steady progress and the excitement of practical implications, neural networks took a back seat due to a paper published at that time. It challenged the ability of networks to advance to a state of having multiple layers. Additionally, researchers and developers made use of an imperfect learning function, which stunted progress. This was detrimental to the research, which affected funding. While many were afraid that the study was dying, knowledge can only be held back so long before something new happens to jolt it forward once more.

The 1970s offered little advancement, except for the development of the first multilayered network by Kunihiko Fukushima. At this point, scientists continued to work in private on solving elemental problems of networks. Some of these researchers included: Grossberg, J.A. Anderson, von der Malsburg, Fukushima, and Kohonen. Their work paid off in the early 1980s.

1980s

In 1982, John Hopfield introduced a system using bidirectional lines; meaning information could travel both ways along a neural network as compared to the former Feedforward net. This same year, a conference on cooperative/competitive neural networks was held between the United States and Japan. Japan announcing a new fifth-generation approach to neural networks was a concern to the United States fearing they could be left behind in the field. The U.S. press went wild. The term fifth generation in computer science denotes the ability of a machine to possess artificial intelligence. This fear motivated restored interest in the field which included restored funding.

In 1986, three groups of researchers set out on a mission to perfect the manner in which machines could learn. They all devised a similar technique, which is now referred to as a backward propagating network. While this approach worked, it is important to note, that backward propagation networks are slow to learn often requiring multiple iterations to become trained.

1990s

Ray Kurzweil dominated in exploiting the practical applications of neural networks during this time. Using the Kurzweil 3000 speech recognition and text to speech software, this was the first profound experience many had with neural network technology. The software's accuracy even stands up to speech recognition software found in modern day.

In his book "The Age of Spiritual Machines" written in 1999, Ray predicts that computers will surpass human experts regarding highest profit investment decisions.

Future

One of the past and present limitations is the hardware that hosts a neural network. Processor speeds of modern computers are still largely insufficient to give rise to highly sophisticated systems capable of providing a timely training process. While processors and graphics processing units (GPUs) are improving, neural network engineers are currently investigating the feasibility of using light instead of digital signals to carry information along the network. It is believed that using light has tremendous implications with regards to calculating complex matrix multiplication problems, which is essential to how neural networks derive resulting outputs.

One of the points this book will make is the need to conceive of new concepts to power the field. The hardware is a considerable component of a neural network. It hosts the neural network that we create inside it. The current problem that is trying to overcome is that modern deep thinking nets require tremendous processing power to train and operate. Instead of pushing the limits of the hardware elements of a neural network, let's begin to generate ideas about how to optimize or design something entirely different.

As you can see, neural networks have fought their ways through history. While they've been tough functions to perfect and stabilize, the human desire for automation and assistance with menial tasks keeps the fire burning. In the next chapter, we will examine how neural networks simulate thinking, learning, and intelligence. You will be presented with crucial insights pertaining to network thought logic.

Computer Thinking

"Everybody right now, they look at the current technology, and they think, 'OK, that's what artificial neural nets are.' And they don't realize how arbitrary it is. We just made it up! And there's no reason why we shouldn't make up something else." - **Geoffrey Hinton**

What really is artificial intelligence? What is the difference between machine learning and deep learning? Let's start with artificial intelligence because that one tends to depend on whom you ask. The word has different shades of meaning depending on context as well.

Some interpretations of the term artificial intelligence referred to a machine that has a general awareness and can engage in many tasks and conversations. These types of machines are only theoretical at this time, remaining in the realm of science fiction. Anytime you may hear someone speak of attaining artificial intelligence as though it has not yet been reached, contextually, this suggests they may be referring to artificial intelligence in the nature previously described.

The second concept of artificial intelligence refers to any task a machine can perform that would normally require a human intelligence to fulfill. Conversely, machines and software fitting this description are widely in use today.

Many times when we hear the term artificial intelligence in use, the second concept or definition of artificial intelligence is what is being discussed. If you are being formal, however, there is a better way to make a distinction between the two. You can imagine why this became necessary.

The term "general artificial intelligence" refers to machines that exhibit awareness and can engage in a variety of tasks. "Narrow artificial intelligence" denotes machine intelligence that can perform a specialized task.

What then is machine learning? Machine learning is the process of feeding data into a neural network so it can better predict a correct result. This is also known as training. When a neural network is adequately trained through some process of machine learning, it may then be referred to as possessing narrow artificial intelligence. There are a few different machine learning techniques being used to train neural networks, so it's useful to understand that the term machine learning is a broad one.

Deep learning, on the other hand, is a bit more specific. Deep learning is a type of machine learning that powers many of the artificial intelligence we use today. It's known for its power and sophistication yielding some of the most intelligent networks created. Deep neural networks earn this classification when a network contains multiple hidden layers. Deep learning just refers to the process of training such a network.

Many people, at first, seem to become slightly disoriented around the definitions of artificial intelligence, machine learning, and deep learning. Just remember that there is more in common than there is to distinguish, but just to put it into perspective one final time: deep learning is one of the many types of machine learning used to train deep neural networks. When adequately trained, these neural networks give rise to a form of artificial intelligence known as narrow artificial intelligence.

Neural networks largely operate simply by multiplying matrices. No, your computer is not thinking of an answer; it is just multiplying one matrix with another and getting a new matrix as the answer. Of course, a sophisticated neural network is calculating thousands, millions, or billions of multiplication problems, but this is all in a nutshell. Now that you understand what a neural network is doing from a technical/mathematical stance, let's examine the visual/graphical side of a neural network.

A neural network accepts input. Input is simply what we want to feed into the system so that it can supply us with a result. A typical example of this could be a photo, video, or speech. As it feeds this information through the layers of its system, it starts to piece together its resulting output. This, in essence, is achieved by sorting. How does a neural network sort something out? It scores probabilities - almost like casting a vote. These votes are combined to establish a sort of confidence rating, or simply put, how certain the network is of its result. Your network will be running your inputs through a series of checks establishing what is absent and present in the input data. It says to itself "this is present, so there is a 62% chance that it is this," or "this is absent, so there's a 78% chance it's not this."

Unless you have a theoretically perfect network, the result will always be the network's best guess. That's right, even a sophisticated and highly trained network doesn't definitively know that it made the correct classification based on the input provided. We can improve the network's system for storing input data by "training the network," which will be further described later. As a neural network progresses through training, it achieves greater success. The most powerful and sophisticated systems can achieve 99.79% accuracy. Why not 100%? We've all been taught that computers are perfect, right? Let's remind ourselves that the computer or network, isn't actually thinking and identifying. A neural network is only a complex math problem - a conceptual design to solve a problem using mathematical means.

However, what if we design a network that can think to a similar degree or quality as the human mind? Could we then achieve 100% accuracy scores? This is a great question. Ask yourself how many times you have misread a word or asked someone to repeat him or herself because you were unsure of a word or words from their sentence. Humans do not have an accurate system for classifying these inputs. That being said, we also don't look at the world around us and classify objects with a passive certainty. The human mind is subjectively sure of the things it observes. This means if I show you a coffee mug, you say "I know that is a coffee mug," while your network will say, "87% coffee mug, 10% grain silo, 2% winter day."

One of the aspects of this topic that makes Artificial Neural Networks so compelling is that their architecture is inspired by the human brain. When you see something, neurons fire up to help you understand the visible world. When someone calls your name, neurons fire up. For every sound you hear, in fact, neurons are firing. Your mind is an interconnected web of information and ideas, with the ability to adjust, improve, and explore. From the time you are born, your mind begins accumulating data. Connecting one experience to another, we learn about how to identify and engage in the world around us. This is the basic model for the human mind as it's applied. The mind learns so it may predict. The sum of all that you have learned gives rise to a being that is capable of cooperating in this sensory existence. We participate in the physical world using predictions to guide our every move. Have you ever considered such a concept? It is true that life is a series of decisions. Everything you say, do, and think is a decision. What motivates our decisions?

This news may seem a bit dull. When you set your alarm at night, how do you decide when to wake up? You deploy your imagination to make a prediction. Our imagination is where we formulate our predictions.

Your coworker sends you a message saying the morning meeting is at 8 AM. You imagine the tasks needed to prepare you for this meeting. You imagine how long you will need to rest, feed yourself, complete your morning routine, and travel to your meeting. You derive these time estimates from past learning. You combine these estimates and confidently set your alarm for 5:30 AM.

Have you ever been late for a morning meeting? This was due to an improper prediction of the time needed. Was it the train's fault you say? Sometimes we are exposed to unforeseen circumstances like the train - information that was not within our scope of evaluation. However, what if you were to be late the following Mondays, would you be blaming this same morning train? Your colleagues would wonder why you haven't learned the train's schedule in order to adjust yours.

Certain predictions you may be highly sure of, like going out in the rain without an umbrella will likely cause you to get wet. Other predictions may be more of an educated guess, for instance, a doctor deciding on a suitable treatment for a patient's illness. All of these are applications of learned information.

Imagine the tool used by criminal investigators in the movies. We typically see a corkboard with photos, newspaper clippings, locations on a map, and other relevant samples and details from the crime. There are strings stretched from one piece of data to the other, indicating they are related in some way. This is a great visual model for how neurons connect to make predictions in both biology and computer science.

This chapter teaches us that neural networks simulate thinking by scoring an input's elemental parts, then returning a multitude of most likely matches. We learned that even a well-trained network is not sure of its responses. This is no fault of the networks, rather a problem to be addressed by future engineers. The human mind doesn't evaluate the characteristics of what he sees and says, "maybe I'm seeing this... or it could be this." On the contrary, if I show you an object, you will not only accurately classify it, but you will be certain. If I tell you, "no, it's not a coffee mug, it's a lamp," you would debate me. This is what is meant by subjective certainty. What is the current difference between human thinking and computer thinking? It's more than a matter of context awareness, GPU speeds, training methods, or the fine-tuning of hyperparameters.

Neural networks critically think about every problem that is given to them. We've created them to be this way. With human learning, we reach a state where learned information is practically memorized. As you read the words on this page, you are retrieving memories of what each word is. You are not decoding each word, and no one could come and uproot your knowledge of these words, as you are subjectively certain of what you are reading.

If I were to present you with some English word you have never seen before, only then, would you similarly evaluate and classify with some passive level of certainty? In that case, someone may come behind you and correct you on that word, and after that one-time training, you are subjectively certain of that word.

Questions

- What does the term "general artificial intelligence" refer to?

- What is machine learning?

- At what point will a neural network produce facts as opposed to guesses?

Components of a Neural Network

"I envision some years from now that the majority of search queries will be answered without you actually asking. It'll just know this is something that you're going to want to see." - **Ray Kurzweil**

I have mentioned in both the "Origin" and "Computer Thinking" chapters some of the elements that make up a neural network. Let's have an overview of everything involved.

Neural networks can perform many tasks that normally require human intelligence:

- Understanding spoken words, or better, the context of words within a sentence

- Identification of objects or faces and features in photo or video

- Matching of similar musical compositions

- Triumph in both board and video games alike

Neural networks can be trained in these capacities along with many others. In 2018, none of these examples are obscure or beyond our reach. Siri, Pandora, Facebook, and Mar i/o are great, accessible examples of deep thinking neural networks. Neural networks can have a very basic and non-sophisticated structure, or they can be complex with many layers that information is processed through. We call this deep thinking or deep neural networks.

How is this information perceived by the system? How does a neural network see, say, an image so it can begin processing it?

Nodes or neurons are the first point of contact and the most primary element of a neural network. Data nodes in an artificial neural network are inspired by the neurons in the human body. The quantity of nodes in a neural network suggests how intelligent that network likely is; however, nodes are not too complex themselves. A data node simply stores a number. Think of it as a memory cell.

How are these nodes organized? You will see in graphical models of neural networks that nodes are stacked in columns. There can be few or many nodes contained in one of these stacks. These stacks of nodes are considered a layer. A neural network will always have an input layer, an output layer, and at least one hidden layer.

The input layer is the aforementioned ability to see by the network. So if we know an input layer is simply some stack of nodes, how does this relate to seeing? Traditionally, a neural network that examines visual data will be engineered to correspond one node with one (usually) tiny part of the image. And so on, each section of the image is given a node which examines only what is happening at that point. It's useful to think of this system as operating the inverse way that a monitor outputs data to us. As for a digital display, images are presented on the screen via a dense grid of pixels. Pixels are merely tiny colored dots but joined together, they seamlessly form a recognizable image to the human eye. Again, let's reverse this system. An input layer, in this case, would note the color or value of each pixel and record that data vertically among the corresponding input nodes. This recorded data serves as the "activation values" for our input layer. The input layer then passes each of its activation values along to the next layer of nodes to begin the process of analyzing this input information.

This processing layer of nodes is known as a "hidden layer." A hidden layer is where a single aspect of analysis takes place in a network. It's where the network "thinks" about its answer.

The number of neurons in these hidden layers can vary depending on how we want our network to process the information it receives. Deciding on a number of nodes in any layer is a matter of network structure.

In the case of a network type called a "convolutional net," there also exists two additional types of hidden layers. A "convolution layer" convolves image data making a digital map of its features. Basically, it is a type of hidden layer that stores images. Pooling layers reduce the resolution of these saved images in an effort to optimize the performance of the network.

The output layer of a neural network is where we receive the results from the network. It will have as many nodes as there are possible classifications. Meaning, each neuron on the output layer has a corresponding label. The neuron with the highest activation value represents the network's choice regarding the current input. It is likely that other nodes in this layer contain activation values that are comparable and perhaps not far from the highest ranking output neuron. Optimally, a network will provide a high activation value for the classification it believes to be most correct, while the other output neurons have a low activation value. A network that can properly classify input with a high contrast between activation values on the output layer would be a very well-trained network.

This is a brief introduction of how a node functions and how nodes are stacked together to form layers in a neural network. We understand the neural aspect of a neural network, now let's proceed to the second half of its name.

The term "network" implies interconnection. What is the connecting aspect within neural networks? These are called "weights." You will see them graphically represented by a line connecting two nodes. Weights correlate the strength or relevance between two nodes. Some networks adjust their weight values each time they receive input to improve the accuracy of their predictions. If the weighted value between two nodes is weak, this suggests that the one node is not strongly related to the other. Likewise, a strong weighted value between two nodes suggests that the two are likely related to solving the task at hand.

The final basic component to these intelligent systems is called biases. I will go a bit more in depth in a later chapter, but it is always important to understand that functionally, biases set a threshold for how strong a connection from a certain previous node should be to receive consideration by the network. It helps the neural network assign relevance to a particular connection.

Questions

- What are four commonplaces of examples of deep thinking neural networks?

- Name the extra hidden layers in a convolutional net neural network?

- How many nodes does the average output layer have?

Nodes

Nodes are the neural part of our neural network. Data nodes, just like the name sounds, are where information is stored and applied within our network. Many types of data can be represented inside a neural network. However, it's important to remember that this information, as the network applies it, is just a number. Maybe you find yourself starting to get lost anytime you conceptualize how numbers relate to solving real-world problems. Don't get hung up. As previously mentioned, the numbers in a neural network are merely representations. Representations could be simple, like black = "0", and white = "1", or a node activation value of "0.86" on some hypothetical hidden layer that could represent the presence of some particular curved line in some image being exposed to our network

Think of the popular music streaming service Pandora. You submit an upvote, a downvote, or no vote at all. This is very similar to how data is carried across a neural network. The node or neuron, will receive an input, formulate a new value, then send out a result or output. When you log into Pandora, select a playlist and start listening, you enter into a system nearly identical to the structure of a neural network. Let's compare. A song plays, and the result is you either like, dislike, or feel neutral about the song playing. To start, let's just think about the up and downvoting. We know that if we submit an upvote, we are indicating to Pandora that the song playing is a strong match to our tastes. Inversely, a downvote indicates the song playing is a poor match. Nodes also use this method to pass along information. Inside a neural network, "upvotes" are indicated with a number "1". "Downvotes" send out a "0". As for the place in the metaphor, describing "no vote" is the technical equivalence to being okay with the song. The node submits a value of "0.5".

Now let's take this a step further. Though it would be much more of a hassle, Pandora would be able to learn of our tastes more efficiently if we were able to submit something that's percentage based. In that case, we would submit a score based on a particular song's match to our styles. "Thirty-four percent match, seventy percent match..."

To review, the key details to remember as a metaphorical reference are:

- "Upvotes" represent a positive "1".

- "Downvotes" represent "0".

- "No vote" represents a "0.5".

- The song playing represents input.

- The vote you submit represents output.

- The song playing compares to your musical preference, just as input combines with node value to derive a resulting output – your vote.

- Your musical preference won't change drastically, or perhaps at all, from song to song. The same applies to the value of a node.

You now understand that a neuron listens, determines, and then votes, just like you do when streaming music, but again, let's add just a bit more detail to this concept of a node. You may be thinking, "Oh that's simple. Just three voting signals to distinguish." Let's remember the nature of numbers in mathematics because this principle is in play within a neural network. There exists a limitless quantity of infinitesimally small numbers lying between "0" and "1". In other words, placing additional zeros directly behind a decimal point in math gives you a dramatically smaller number to the same degree that adding zeros in front of the decimal on your paycheck would.

Neural network engineers and enthusiasts refer to the output value submitted by a node as the node's activation. So a node value of "1" would mean that the node is active. A node value of 0.5 is moderately active. A node value of 0 means the node is inactive.

A node's activation value is multiplied with the node's weight in a neural network to determine the information being sent to the next layer of receiving nodes. Right before it leaves as output, a value called "bias" is added.

All of these numbers being multiplied and added must result in output values greater than "1" sometimes, right? And if the bias value happens to be negative, wouldn't we encounter results smaller than "0"? Absolutely, we do. Yet how can these quantities exist inside a function based only on values between "1" and "0"? Traditionally, they cannot. How do we make use of values larger than "1" and smaller than "0" with a neural net? If you were working with a neural network that uses "binary values," then one way would be to run these numbers we are trying to pass along through a "sigmoid activation function." If you've taken a statistics class, you also understand this to be a 'logistic curve.'

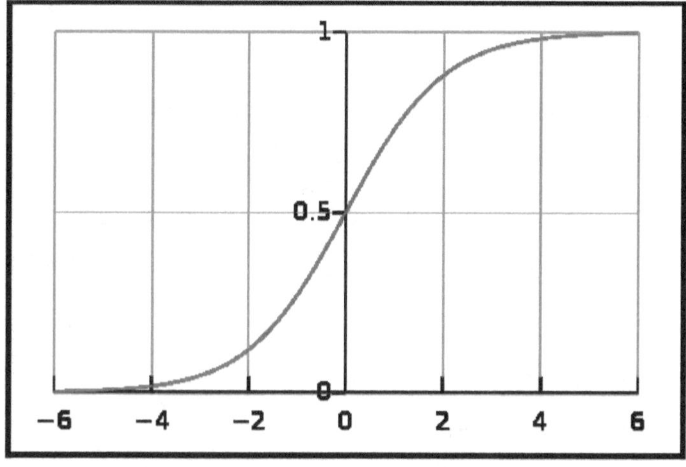

Graphing a logistic curve provides a great visual representation of how the sigmoid activation function compresses values. At the topmost section of the graph, we see the curve begin to approach "1," however it never quite arrives at 1. Likewise, the bottom of the curve never completely reaches "0". You have probably noticed that to the left, and right we have the number line which represents the number we are putting into the function. Again, this is the value we need to compress between "1" and "0". The output of the function is represented along the vertical axis. Using this image as a guideline, we can see that inputting "1" into the sigmoid function would return a value around "0.75". Looking at this model helps us understand what's occurring in the function from a visual perspective, but its functionality is very limited if you want to input numbers larger than 1. A computer uses the formula $F(x)=1/1+e^{-x}$ to reach a precise answer.

There are a few other activation functions we can use within our networks. While sigmoid activation function is classically taught, it is less often used in modern day neural networks. The next most popular activation function in network training is ReLU.

ReLU is an activation function expressed as: $A(x) = \max(0, x)$. ReLU stands for rectified linear units. This activation function has become popular due to its ability to train networks more efficiently as compared to networks trained with sigmoid. With ReLU, any negative number passed into the function will be output as "0". Positive numbers input into the function will return the same value. Positive numbers adhere to the identity function when using ReLUs. Since values less than zero are expressed as zero in the network, far fewer neurons are active during the firing process. This gives rise to a more efficient training process, as sigmoid activated networks feature many more activations during each iteration. The more node activations a network has, the costlier that network is to run. ReLUs are best used with deep neural networks because of the many nodes and layers contained within them. A drawback of ReLU activated networks is that the loss of values smaller than zero contributes to an issue known as the dying ReLU problem. Not factoring negative quantities into the equation essentially contributes to a loss of data. It is common for a network using ReLUs to have multiple "dead neurons." A high number of non-firing neurons renders a sizable portion of the network passive. You could say the benefit of ReLU is also the problem.

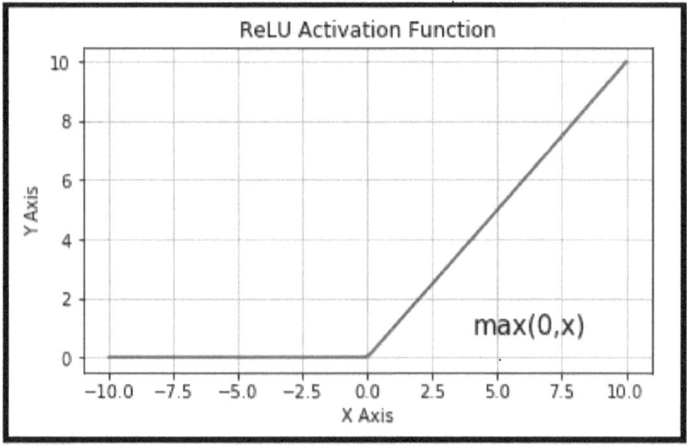

Again, zero or any value less than zero returns zero. Any value greater than zero returns that same value by the ReLU activation function.

Questions

- What methods do nodes use to pass along information?

- When someone is discussing a node's activation, to what are they referring?

- Besides ReLU, what is the most popular activation function?

Layers

"People understand the linear algebra behind deep learning [neural networks]. But the models it produces are less human-readable. They're machine-readable. They can retrieve very accurate results, but we can't always explain, on an individual basis, what led them to those accurate results." - **Chris Nicholson**

We already understand that a layer is some stack of nodes. Layers are represented mathematically using a matrix-vector. Why is this appropriate? Using a matrix-vector to mathematically express a layer in a neural network works well because the nature in which data is structured in a network layer is identical to how values are structured in a matrix-vector. If we have a simple layer with 3 nodes possessing activation values of 2, 7, and -3, we would just stack these values vertically and wrap them in brackets to convert the layer into a matrix-vector.

You will typically see neural networks laid out in a left to right format. Leftmost is a column of nodes called the input layer. This is where we feed information into our neural network. Nodes are graphically represented by a small circle. The illustration may also have a number appearing inside the circle. This number, again, is the activation value for that node. A great way to think of this input layer would be to liken it to the optic nerve in your eye. The optic nerve receives raw, physical data of the light that is entering your eye. It doesn't know what it's looking at, that's for the brain to decide. Its task is only to relay an impulse about what is (and isn't) there.

You just learned that the input layer is like the eyes of the network. You can think of the hidden layers of a network as the place where the information is processed. This is where the magic of a neural network happens.

Hidden layers in a neural network are where our network thinks about the problem it's trying to solve. If the input layer breaks what we feed into the system into tiny parts spread across the neurons of that input layer, the hidden layers' task is to re-assemble these parts into something coherent to the system. It is possible for a neural network to contain only one hidden layer. However, this network would have limited functionality. As many of the neural networks we use today are striving to achieve a type of artificial intelligence, many hidden layers are required. It is best to expect the neural networks you encounter now, and going forth, to contain multiple hidden layers. When you have many hidden layers in a neural network, the network is then referred to as a deep network.

There are also especially hidden layers called "pooling" and "convolution" layers, and are found in a network type called "convolutional neural networks." This book will give a more detailed description of what they are and how they work in the "Net Types" chapter. For now, remember convolutions layers store images and pooling layers lower the resolution of these stored images. A convolution layer is usually followed by a pooling layer in a network.

Multiple hidden layers featured in more intelligent networks are appropriate due to the nature in which hidden layers process information for the whole. Each layer of a neural network works to pick up patterns received by the previous layer reconstructing the input piece by piece. A layer does not create one result, but many possible pattern arrangements and configurations. These reconstructions are what is being voted on as it is passed along the network.

This brings us to the final layer type contained in a neural network.

Output layers are the final destination of both our input and hidden layers. An output layer contains as many nodes as there are classification labels. If we want the network to generate a response based on ten possible outputs, the output layer will have ten nodes. Likewise, if we want the network to distinguish between many classifications, say over two-hundred, there will be over two-hundred nodes on this output layer as well. At the point our input has progressed through the network reaching the output layer, the voting process has reached its consensus. Yes, in the end, a network's response to the input provided is the node on the output layer with the highest activation. This is what the network deems the correct answer to be. This is where the scoring of probabilities comes in. Understand that if, for example, an output layer is outfitted with twenty neurons, the neural network will actually return twenty responses. It doesn't look for the one right answer as we do; it considers and scores the probability that the input was perhaps any of the known outputs. Do you see the room for improvement being suggested? Is it the different contextual awareness or is it much deeper than that?

This book emphasizes deep and convolutional networks, but it's also worth learning that some neural networks are not laid out from left to right. Recursive Neural Tensor Networks (RNTN), for example, exhibit a hierarchal structure. So convolutional networks feature a graphical representation resembling a spider's web, while RNTNs share resemblances to a tree.

Questions

- Why is the matrix-vector a natural fit for representing layers?

- How does a network choose which answer is the correct answer?

- In what way is the average neural network laid out?

Training and Back Propagation

"One reason I'm not worried about the possibility that we will soon make machines that are smarter than us is that we haven't managed to make machines until now that are smart at all. Artificial intelligence isn't synthetic intelligence: It's pseudo-intelligence." - **Alva Noe**

The ability for a network to train is the distinguishing mark between conventional computer programming and computer programs capable of machine learning. Currently, networks require a lot of time to train their connections in order to successfully solve the problems we feed them. Does the human mind process information faster than modern-day hardware or do training models and net structures need to fundamentally change? As you discover how neural networks rewrite themselves in order to supply us with a high volume of correct answers, begin to consider the way learning happens inside your mind.

"Backwards propagation" is a popular network training technique. Before we proceed deeper into this concept, let's start by understanding a fundamental truth about the backward propagation technique. Backward propagation is calculating and adjusting derivative values. When a network misclassifies an input, it is a measure of numerically how wrong the network was generated. With this number, we can do something interesting to simulate learning.

Imagine that you believe you've found your ideal companion. After meeting several times at a local smoothie shop and engaging in some pleasant conversation, you are convinced that you want to see this person beyond your smoothie shop encounters and schedule a real first date. You determine that you should be able to maintain the interest of this ideal companion if you can represent to her that you are indeed a perfect match. Demonstration of your compatibility has become your function. You set some initial ideas about your identity within this blossoming relationship and how you expect it to perform. Before you know it, the night of your first date arrives. Your attraction has you feeling nervous. Additionally, as the host is escorting you to your table, a passing waiter accidentally splashes your outfit with some wine. Classic. Despite this, you are eager to discover similarities between you and her. You ask many questions throughout the night and find she has a variety of interests, however, many aren't alike to yours. The food is excellent, best in town, but it's not until the last bites of your entrée that you notice you've been chewing with your mouth open the entire time.

After dessert and two glasses of wine, your nerves have receded and you feel free to share a wealth of information about yourself. Halfway through your story about getting lost during your first hunting trip, she excuses herself saying she must get some rest before her big day tomorrow. What's happening tomorrow you wonder? Of all things discussed, she never mentioned anything special occurring tomorrow. You consider the possibility that you perhaps talked too much not giving her enough conversational space to get around to current affairs. You fear you have turned her off. You continue to analyze the results from the night and surmise that wearing a soiled garment and your new found talent of uncovering the dissimilarities in your personal interests have all contributed to a less than ideal first date. You tally four errors and commit to resolving them if there is the next date. She calls you three days later (not bad) and sets up a time to meet again with you next week. Now is your chance to avert the mistakes from last time in an effort to attend a date with zero errors.

You're a computer programmer after all and delivering sophisticated solutions and debugging problems is your thing. Being more self-aware and armed with a rough formula for success, you attend your second date. Your second date returns three errors, an improvement, though still a departure from your expectation. You continue this pattern of totaling up errors committed on these dates. Time after time, you reduce your error score, yet you are dissatisfied with the inefficiency of your approach. Your dates are becoming a bit better each time, but you decide multiple average dates costs a lot of time and energy, which threatens to become inconvenient and unfeasible if this rate is sustained. It's apparent that if you can't accelerate this decent toward zero errors, a new method of achieving your initial goal (uncovering the match) must be employed.

After some deep evaluation of the situation and some introspection, you identify a small change that will make a big difference. You retire your harsh and self-critical ways of noting and obsessing to avoid errors in favor of a model that spotlights the positive aspects of your dates. You now both initiate and attend your dates with a mindset of "I play to win." Congratulations. You just retired a technique known as "backward propagation" in favor of a learning model called "reinforcement learning."

It has already been explored if backward propagated networks were intuitive at all, or they operate essentially to memorize their training data. Intuitively, doesn't it seem that we should be programming our machines to find the best-fit solution, rather than centering its system on errors?

The use of backward propagation also calls for an understanding of the mathematical concept of linear regression or gradient descent. Linear regression is a more specific term describing what is happening during the backpropagation process. Our network tries to devise a model that will best fit the data that it's trying to classify. It's a complicated concept that should really be demonstrated visually, but as that is outside of the capabilities of this eBook, let's just remember the following. Linear regression is the process of locating the best model for classifying our data using gradient descent.

It is possible to essentially over-train your network. This is known as "overfitting." Again, this is concept is best portrayed visually, but having a model that overfits the data the network must analyze, reduces the networks accuracy. This is because overfitting creates a model that is too descriptive and thereby restrictive. This is similar to entering a search query that is too specific disabling the search engine's ability to display relevant search results.

Backward propagation and reinforcement learning are two methods neural networks engineers employ to train machines. Backward propagation is the name of your first approach to winning the returned interest of your date. While it seemed like she liked you regardless, your strategy was to avoid upsetting her, messing up, and doing the wrong thing. At the end of each date, you totaled up your missteps or "errors" to determine what is called a "cost score." Your cost score is the sum of these errors.

A network takes its cost score and refeeds it through the neural network making internal adjustments to its own rules on how to handle the input. But where does the network apply adjustments within itself to affect the resulting output? With each iteration, the network delivers its adjustments to an element of the neural network called weights.

Metaphorically, each date from our story would be considered a different iteration. With a neural network, each time the input to output cycle runs its course, the network has completed an iteration. With each iteration, a neural network becomes a bit smarter through the use of the backward propagation process.

Reinforcement learning changes the equation to favor a high scoring value. The score value in this training structure is called a "reward signal." These networks pursue the action that will greatly improve the current state. Learning takes place through the interaction of the agent within the environment. Networks using this method, build their connections rather than going back and modifying them. Depending on the problem you want your network to solve, reinforcement learning can be a powerful training method and should be strongly considered. It has given new life to the world of Artificial Intelligence and Machine Learning.

The terms supervised and unsupervised learning refer to the nature in which we train our network. Supervised learning is a network training type that features the use of labeled training data. This means we provide our network with training examples so it can begin familiarizing itself with consistent patterns in a labeled dataset. Our network improves and progresses as it's exposed to increasingly diverse sets of training data. This training type is best suited to networks being applied toward classification functions. Data being "labeled," just means applying and accompanying label or name, to the information we wish to expose to the network.

Networks trained using the unsupervised learning approach work to find hidden structure using unlabeled data. An example of data that is unlabeled is demographical information. Information we would like to evaluate and even forecast needs not to be labeled. Being that the data is unlabeled, there is no error or reward signal generated by the network. This training type is best suited to networks being applied in data and statistical analysis.

Additionally, there is semi-supervised learning. It is applying in the same fashion as networks using a supervised learning method. The key difference is these networks are exposed to a combination of labels and unlabeled data during the training process. Large quantities of labeled data can be cost-prohibitive. In this case, a network may be engineered to accept both types.

Questions

- What separates the average computer program from a program that is capable of machine learning?

- What is backwards propagation?

- How can you avoid overfitting?

Weights and Biases

"The history of AI research, which can be traced back 58 years to a conference at Dartmouth College in New Hampshire where the phrase was coined, has been littered with false dawns. If the latest hopes also fall short, it won't be because of a lack of ambition or effort." - **Richard Waters**

Weights are a value representation of how strong the connection between one node is with another. They establish a score based on relevance. How relevant is information "A," to information "B?" Their degree of relevance is the weighted value. This is graphically portrayed as a line connecting two nodes. In more detailed illustrations, you will see these lines represented by different shades in the grayscale spectrum or even shades of color.

As with the layers of a neural network, we will also express our weighted values in a matrix. At this point since we know that weight values are multiplied by activation values, we begin to see just why a neural network is only a matter of solving a detailed matrices multiplication operation. We will resume talking about weights for now, but I'm sure you might have an idea how biases will be mathematically expressed and factored to with the other network elements.

The value of weights will change over the course of the learning or training process. This is an adjustment that the network makes to itself, however, one adjustment that you have at your disposal is a parameter called learning rate. Learning rate defines a speed at which we would like the network to learn. However, it is more of a threshold indicating how much the network is allowed to adjust its weights each time it is exposed to information or training data. You still may not see how this is more than an adjustment of speed. Why not just set the learning rate parameter value high and train your network overnight? While a book cannot present an interactive model of a network being trained for demonstration purposes, it is important that you understand that as the learning rate increases, information becomes lost concerning how to work out the problem. It's a loss of the finer details. It is probable that setting the learning rate high will render your network useless altogether. A good analogy would be if you began vigorously studying Mandarin in hopes of passing an advanced usage test in three days. Obviously, the error in this approach is that an accelerated rate of learning afforded you less of an ability to examine the finer details that give rise to the broader scope of understanding. Smaller learning rate values increase the resolution of the learning process. As we all know, high-resolution means longer processing times. Many hyperparameters are a matter of fine-tuning.

Remember back to an earlier chapter where I presented the example of setting the alarm for the morning meeting? Our hypothetical character probably had his weights configured to prioritize an on-time arrival very low. When weight values in a region of a neural network are small, or "not strongly weighted," that means the data stored in the corresponding node is rated with a low relevance. In other words, the connected information is not that important to the question the network is trying to solve. To compare back to the story, our meeting attendee doesn't really care that much about getting to the meeting. Perhaps, he cared a bit more the first time, but after he was late consecutive times without reprimand, he learned to assign less importance with regards to being on time. "It's not important," his neural network says. "Catching up on the latest news and enjoying the taste of this morning coffee is a priority over leaving early to beat the train." It sounds like our character trains his network using reinforcement learning. I concur.

A bias in a neural network is an additional device used to help prioritize data being passed along. As with the other components, biases are a number. They can be any number and one of the variables a network adjusts as it trains itself. You can use many metaphors to make this concept relatable. I like to envision a "must be this tall to ride" meter. If you don't measure up to the minimum height requirement, you will not even be considered to board that ride. Okay, so if a bias is how tall you must be in order to be considered, what metaphorically compares to a rider's height? With this example, weights are the symbolic reference. We already know that weights are the lines that connect one node to another and they carry a value representing how related two nodes are to each other. Now the bias enters in, establishing a numerical standard for what that weighted value ought to be. It's regarded as a pre-output adjustment. You will also see a bias being graphically represented as a hidden, independent node from the rest of the visible network structure.

To review: The neural network sums the weight value and the bias value to formulate the activation value of the receiving node. A node's activation value is multiplied with the node's weight in a neural network to determine the information being sent to the next layer of receiving nodes. Right before it leaves as output, a value called "bias" is added.

Questions

- How is the weighted value for two nodes determined?

- The speed at which we would like the network to learn is called what?

- At what point do biases come into play?

Net Types and Best Applications

"In the past, Google has used teams of humans to 'read' its street address images - in essence, to render images into actionable data. But using neural network technology, the company has trained computers to extract that data automatically - and with a level of accuracy that meets or beats human operators." - **John Battelle**

For a majority of the book so far, we have used a network type known as a feedforward net as the model for helping us understand how most neural networks work. Now is the time to build a bit more onto some of the information you've acquired so far. Not all neural networks feature the same components. Some of the neural network types described below introduce new elements. There are many other network types that are not shared in this chapter and hopefully, much more waiting to be created by you! All of these network types have specific specializations that may make deciding on an appropriate network structure.

Feedforward Neural Network

Feedforward networks operate in the manner outlined so far in this book. As the name implies, these networks pass information in a forward direction from layer to layer. Nodes don't form a cycle in this system. This system is typically illustrated from left to right, with the input layer at the leftmost part of the illustration and output node at the right extreme end. This is a simple system to understand and also the first type of neural network invented. It is a forward propagating network with no backpropagation. Feedforward nets can be applied in speech recognition and image processing.

Recurrent Neural Network (RNN)

The principle distinction with a recurrent neural network is, as the name implies, information recurs. RNN, for short, features a structure similar to Feedforward nets. Information travels one direction down the network until it reaches the output layer. The data from the output layer is then re-fed into the system, and the cycle repeats. Since each output is looped back around to the input layer, recurrent neural networks are helpful in creating tools that can predict the next word of a sentence. Smartphone keyboards are a great example of this. Ask yourself, is there a better way for a network to improve its process for predicting a probable proceeding word. RNNs can also be used to analyze video, which lends them the ability to apply toward driverless car systems. However, tech company NVidia employs a convolutional net to power their self-driving system.

Convolutional Neural Network (CNN)

Introduced in 1998, convolutional neural networks are similar to feedforward networks. They excel at tasks involving classification. Convolutional networks examine the elements of their input in small portions. They're great at detecting edges and corners in images in order to distinguish one classification from another. Convolutional networks contain the typical input, output, and fully connected hidden layers; however, they additionally feature especially hidden layers called pooling and convolution layers. As indicated in the name, convolution layers work by convolving an image. In a convolution layer, our network examines portioned features of an image to create a map of data relating to the features contained in the image. We call these feature maps. A pooling layer's role is to compress the resolution of feature maps created by the convolution layer. You can think of this operation as a network creating an abbreviated version of the feature map, so it is easier to process along the rest of the network. Almost like when you see the abbreviation "Jan." The word has been shortened, but there is still enough information for you to understand that we are referring to the month of January. It is also worth mentioning that convolutional networks are known for having what is referred to as sparse interactions. Since all layers are not necessarily fully connected layers, there tends to be less irrelevant neural activity generated. Less neural activity contributes to a more efficient network that is less costly to run. Convolutional neural networks are also applied in speech recognition. Many of their applications of this powerful network type are being explored.

Restricted Boltzmann Machine (RBM)

The Boltzmann Machine, invented by Geoffrey Hinton, is best suited to feature detection and classification in machine learning. RBMs recognize patterns through a reconstruction of input data. These networks have a simple structure consisting of only two layer types, a visible layer, and a hidden layer. These layers are fully connected. Again, fully connected meaning every node from one layer is connected with every node in another. RBMs do not require label data for training. You may remember that this is called unsupervised learning.

Recursive Neural Tensor Network (RNTN)

Recursive Neural Tensor Network are used to explore hierarchical structure in data. A popular application is sentence sentiment analysis. In sentiment analysis, our network must be able to not only pick up on whether the words comprising it are positive or negative, but must also evaluate the order in which they appear in the sentence. RNTNs features a unique structure with its neurons grouped into distinct structures. First, we have the "parent group." Naturally, "child group" is the name of the group extending from a parent group. Child groups are not connected to each other, but only to the parent. This structure forms what is known as a binary tree. As with any network, the number of neurons featured in these groups correlates to the complexity of the data we wish for our network to solve. Data in these networks is processed in a recursive manner. In the case of sentence sentiment analysis, each word of the sentence is placed on a particular node in the child group. The parent group is able to assign both a classifier and score each of the input words. From this, the network is then able to assign each word in a sentence a part of speech (noun, verb, adjective, etc.). Backward propagation is used to train RNTNs. A score is derived from the contrast between the correct sentence structure and the structure of the sentence output by the net.

Questions

- Describe how Feedforward neural networks operate.

- What sets convolutional networks apart from Feedforward networks?

- When is the Recursive Neural Tensor Network most commonly used?

Building a Neural Network

"Artificial intelligence is complex, but creating it is relatively simple. Plop it in a virtual environment, give it a goal, and let it fail and fail and fail until it figures out how to complete the task at hand." - **Dan Seitz**

This book has given you practical and detailed descriptions of the components comprising a neural network. We have also established the scope of their capacity and their present limitations. You can now distinguish between the various types of neural networks currently in use. Having these practical understandings now lends itself to empower you to take the reins.

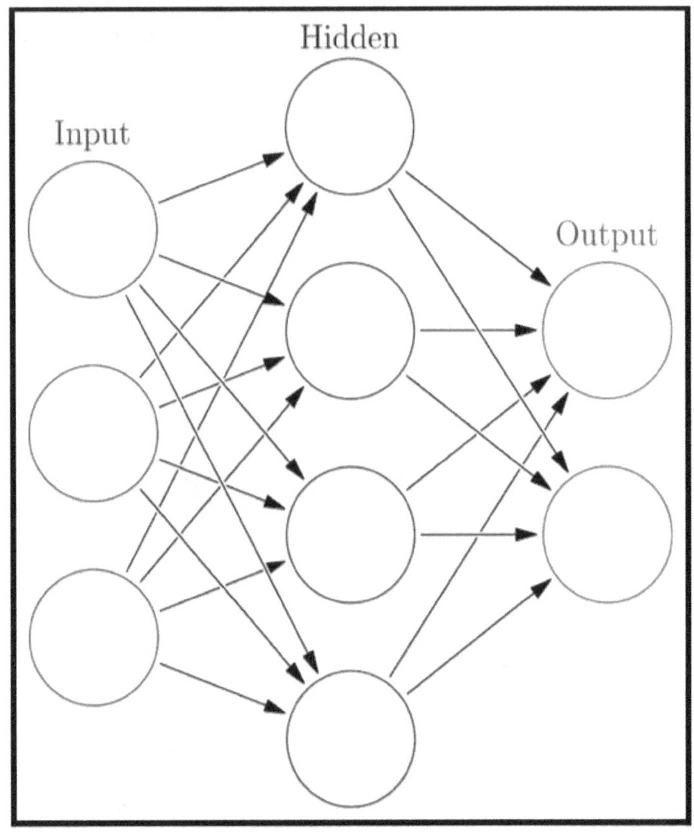

Source: Neural Networks [ONLINE]. Available at:
https://commons.wikimedia.org/wiki/File:Colored_neural_network.svg
[Accessed 28 July 2018]

In the illustration above, we see a depiction of
the neural net elements. This is a very basic

network. At the very left, we have the input layer with three input nodes. This is followed by a hidden layer containing four nodes for processing the input of our network. The final column, containing two nodes, is the output layer. The output nodes themselves are not labeled, but if a network ever exhibits a structure containing two output nodes, we can infer that we are likely seeking a binary response. For example, yes or no, black or white, up or down, etc. Additionally, this image depicts a network where all nodes are connected to every node, directly or indirectly, with each successive layer. When the nodes of one layer connect to each of the nodes of the following layer, we have what is known as a fully connected layer.

Do you remember that neural networks are just complex matrices? From what we understand so far, the nodes in this diagram above would have a number written inside representing that node's activation value. Two numbers are then multiplied together, the activation value with the weight strength. Finally, a bias is added to the product of weight strength and activation value before reaching the next layer of nodes where another round of multiplication and addition takes place.

Each layer of a network is mapped out on its own matrix-vector in this case. The mathematical expression of this entails corresponding your activation values, weighted values, and biases to a matrix, expressing each of the values respectively and how they are to be combined.

Many deep nets usefully connect layers to pass along information and perform a detailed analysis of the input being passed through. While this may allow for a more comprehensive analysis, some may argue that the time, resources, and maintenance required to uphold such a network structure are too costly. Imagine all of the computations the computer would have to solve. With a convolutional net, we escaped this problem, in part, as convolutional nets feature few or no fully connected layers to formulate their output.

Now let's go a step further by applying our knowledge to theorize about an appropriate network structure. This book will not try to coach you on some right way to create your neural network, rather, it will give one final representation of the capabilities of the elements in play.

Input nodes together make up a layer that could be thought of as eyes, ears, or some sensory organ. Anything in the physical world you wish to input into a neural network for analysis can be. First, we need to process the signal for this input. In other words, we must digitize the information. This is simply exploring and deciding on some way to measure and represent the desired input logically.

Existing networks designed to see images do so by simply routing a neuron to a particular place in the image. That one neuron's function is to describe the light information occurring at that one point. This technique is widely used because it is practical and effective. Notice the implicit room for improvement. As humans, we orient to the world around us largely through the use of our eyes. We scan for where visible light is and is not. Dogs tend to use their sense of smell to make sense of their environment. It would take rigorous training to teach a human how to make sense of his environment using his nose, and you can't show a dog a YouTube video of tricks you wish for him to perform.

You should wonder if there are better ways to input image data or any data for that matter into a machine. Is there a type of signal format that networks could process far better than the signals we rely on? Is an input layer even the best way to input data into a machine learning system? If we want to use biology as an inspiration for creating machine intelligence, we should note that input is not processed by neurons. The human body employs nerve cells as the sensory interface between you and the external world. Neurons are tasked with processing this information. Do you see how they are two different workers with two different jobs in biology? This is hardly the case with neural networks as they're currently applied.

When building your neural network, deciding on the number of hidden layers will probably be much easier than deciding on how many nodes a hidden layer should have. The number of hidden layers a network has typically corresponded to the number of evaluations needed to arrive at a result. Again, these layers measure one aspect of the overall problem then formulate a ranking for how relevant each piece of information they were given is to the overall question. The operation entails sorting and filtering. A problem that is growing as conventional neural networks progress is that these networks require a lot of processing power to carry out their functions. This should be no surprise to engineers as a neural network sequentially reviews everything that has been taught when evaluating any given input. Imagine if your mind reviewed every classification type you've ever been introduced to if I showed you a coffee mug.

Deciding on a structure for your output layer will most likely be easiest. The number of neurons in your output layer will be equal to the number of possible outputs you wish for your network to provide you. We know if a network is designed to identify handwritten digits, it is likely there are ten output neurons in that network. If it recognizes handwritten letters of the alphabet, we could infer twenty-six output neurons. Neural networks employing hierarchal structures differ from this, however, have you already been thinking of better possible ways a neural network could indicate a response?

Assigning weight values between nodes can be done manually or set randomly in the initial creation of your network. You may have a choice to predefine or randomizede these values, or your data may dictate randomization. An example where pre-defining weights would be irrelevant is in an unsupervised learning model. Since the data is not labeled in these networks, we're usually asking the network to evaluate patterns in data that may not be apparent to human observers. If you choose to predefine weights in a network that is operating with labeled data, understand that the logic you define in your network to help it arrive at a solution is likely to change. Often, networks completely readjust predefined weight values. What this really means is that the network chooses to solve the problem in a way that is suitable to it despite your initial programming.

Even more fascinating is that we usually cannot intellectualize how these networks achieve accurate results according to the weight values they have set for themselves.

Is it necessary for your network to backtrack in an effort to minimize the chance of making mistakes to achieve correctness? If this is most appropriate for the problem you're trying to solve, then train your network using backward propagation. If you're looking for a bit more natural and intuitive approach, using reinforcement learning to train your network is highly recommended. Compare the similarities between how we learn and how networks train. Consider that the manner in which a network learns will have profound impacts on how it behaves.

TensorFlow is a platform developed by Google to host neural network and machine learning technologies for all. It is easy to use and a highly recommended starting point in your experimentations with networks. TensorFlow's "open source software library" is a very useful environment to become familiar with as its capabilities go beyond the reaches of solely a practice tool. Companies like eBay, Uber, Dropbox, and even Coca-Cola harness the power TensorFlow's resources.

Predecessor DistBelief was a Google brand-exclusive tool based off of deep net technology. It's used in research and production spread across the other Alphabet companies (Alphabet being the parent company of Google) and was improved upon. This gave birth to TensorFlow - a faster, open-source software library.

Before using TensorFlow, it will be necessary to learn Python, which is a programming language. Python is commonly used to code neural networks. Udemy.com offers many courses teaching Python, although Mimo is a great app for picking these concepts up on the go also.

Let's start with these code examples:

To start, you will need to run python and run the following lines to set up your environment:

```
from __future__ import absolute_import
from __future__ import division
from __future__ import print_function

import numpy as np
import tensorflow as tf
```

Layers are a key parameter with regards to network training. We know that a layer is a collection of nodes in a neural network. When we are coding our network, however, a layer will contain weighted sum information and the activation function.

Create a layer using the following code. The result will be a dense layer programmed to take multiple input vectors and return a single output. To add a layer to an input, call the layer as a function.

```
x = tf.placeholder(tf.float32, shape=[None, 3])
linear_model = tf.layers.Dense(units=1)
y = linear_model(x)
```

Layers contain variables that must be initialized before use. While this can be done individually, the following will enable initialization of all variables at once.

```
init = tf.global_variables_initializer()
sess.run(init)
```

Try to incorporate this code last, so it indeed initializes all variables contained within.

Congratulations, you've just started building your first network model! There's more information about layer functions and network training available for free on TensorFlow's website.

The chart below is a glossary for some of the variables you will be working with when you code your network.

Source: Basic Python Network [ONLINE]. Available at: https://iamtrask.github.io/2015/07/12/basic-python-network/ [Accessed 1 August 2018].

Variable	Definition
X	Input dataset matrix where each row is a training example
y	Output dataset matrix where each row is a training example
l0	First Layer of the Network, specified by the input data
l1	Second Layer of the Network, otherwise known as the hidden layer
syn0	First layer of weights, Synapse 0, connecting l0 to l1.
*	Elementwise multiplication, so two vectors of equal size are multiplying corresponding values 1-to-1 to

	generate a final vector of identical size.
-	Elementwise subtraction, so two vectors of equal size are subtracting corresponding values 1-to-1 to generate a final vector of identical size.
x.dot(y)	If x and y are vectors, this is a dot product. If both are matrices, it's a matrix-matrix multiplication. If only one is a matrix, then it's vector-matrix multiplication.

When training your network, you will need a massive amount of training data. Training data is simply a batch of examples similar to what our network was designed to accurately solve. We will use these examples to train the network.

Another, usually smaller, a batch of data used is called test data. While it is a part of the overall training process, test data, is for testing the accuracy of the network as a conclusory step in the training process.

The more training data you have, the higher the accuracy of your network. The more testing data you have available, the better you were able to describe the accuracy of your network. If you have a limited amount of data, it may be necessary to split the pool between testing and training data. Try to reserve at least 10% of the data for testing purposes. It will be necessary to scatter the data as much as possible in both of these sets. Also, you will not want to cross any of the samples from the sets, else you may skew testing results.

It is possible to hack into a neural network. Why would someone want to do this? The reason for hacking remains the same as in other cases. The hacker has some information to gain or wishes to disrupt the system. Some neural networks contain sensitive information that would be considered highly valuable to hackers. Emerging technology like self-driving cars employ neural networks to power this auto-piloted car system. If a hacker retrains these types of networks, he can control principle operational functions, e.g. how to handle the instance of a red light. You can see how the implications here are frightening. This book outlines the known method for hacking a neural network in order to equip you with a deeper understanding of how a neural network operates, while also highlighting its limitations and vulnerabilities.

There are multiple ways to go about hacking a network. One way is to attack the machine learning algorithm for the network. We've learned that a network tasked with classification, for example, examines the tiny details that make up the image and scores them to draw a conclusion about the subject of the image. Using backward propagation, the network learns what each classification is through the process of providing tons of training data to the network over thousands of iterations. With the backward propagated network, the network generates an error score to measure the difference in the network's output classification versus the actual correct image classification. This error score is going to be a key element in tampering with the network.

We will use an image classifying network as the model of how to effectively hack a network. Let's say we want to deceive the network into misclassifying a particular image it has been trained. We first would want to take that image, feed it into the system and note the error score generated with regards to the classification we wish to retrain the system with. Remember, I said this error score would be elemental. Using this error score and the process of backward propagation, we make graphical adjustments to our input photo causing the network to begin favoring the desired classification label that we are trying to set. Once the modified image properly starts to affect the target network, we repeat the process over thousands of iterations. Effectively, this hacking technique exploits the network training process.

It has been recommended to combat this type of hacking, a neural network engineer should include hacked images into the initial training data to render your network impervious to this offense.

The following code will serve as an educational guide and template for you to refer to when coding your first neural networks. The code is written in Python and is supplied by Siraj Raval. There are also walk through tutorials on Google and YouTube available that will explain these lines step by step.

```python
from numpy import exp, array, random, dot

class NeuralNetwork():

    def __init__(self):

        # Seed the random number generator,
so it generates the same numbers

        # every time the program runs.

        random.seed(1)


        # We model a single neuron, with 3
input connections and 1 output connection.

        # We assign random weights to a 3 x 1
matrix, with values in the range -1 to 1

        # and mean 0.

        self.synaptic_weights = 2 *
random.random((3, 1)) - 1
```

```python
        # The Sigmoid function, which describes
an S shaped curve.

        # We pass the weighted sum of the
inputs through this function to

        # normalise them between 0 and 1.

        def __sigmoid(self, x):

            return 1 / (1 + exp(-x))


        # The derivative of the Sigmoid function.

        # This is the gradient of the Sigmoid
curve.

        # It indicates how confident we are about
the existing weight.

        def __sigmoid_derivative(self, x):
```

```python
        return x * (1 - x)


    # We train the neural network through a
process of trial and error.

    # Adjusting the synaptic weights each
time.

    def train(self, training_set_inputs,
training_set_outputs,
number_of_training_iterations):

        for iteration in
xrange(number_of_training_iterations):

            # Pass the training set through our
neural network (a single neuron).

            output =
self.think(training_set_inputs)
```

```
        # Calculate the error (The difference
between the desired output

        # and the predicted output).

        error = training_set_outputs - output


        # Multiply the error by the input and
again by the gradient of the Sigmoid curve.

        # This means less confident weights
are adjusted more.

        # This means inputs, which are zero,
do not cause changes to the weights.

        adjustment =
dot(training_set_inputs.T, error *
self.__sigmoid_derivative(output))


        # Adjust the weights.
```

```python
        self.synaptic_weights += adjustment

    # The neural network thinks.

    def think(self, inputs):

        # Pass inputs through our neural
network (our single neuron).

        return self.__sigmoid(dot(inputs,
self.synaptic_weights))


if __name__ == "__main__":

    #Intialise a single neuron neural
network.

    neural_network = NeuralNetwork()
```

```
        print "Random starting synaptic weights:
"

        print neural_network.synaptic_weights


        # The training set. We have 4 examples,
each consisting of 3 input values

        # and 1 output value.

        training_set_inputs = array([[0, 0, 1], [1,
1, 1], [1, 0, 1], [0, 1, 1]])

        training_set_outputs = array([[0, 1, 1,
0]]).T


        # Train the neural network using a
training set.

        # Do it 10,000 times and make small
adjustments each time.
```

```
neural_network.train(training_set_inputs,
training_set_outputs, 10000)

    print "New synaptic weights after
training: "

    print neural_network.synaptic_weights

    # Test the neural network with a new
situation.

    print "Considering new situation [1, 0, 0]
-> ?: "

    print neural_network.think(array([1, 0,
0]))
```

Neural Networks

Created by Milo Spencer-Harper, the following code generates a basic neural network using far fewer lines of code:

from numpy import exp, array, random, dot

```
    training_set_inputs = array([[0, 0, 1], [1, 1, 1], [1, 0, 1], [0, 1, 1]])

    training_set_outputs = array([[0, 1, 1, 0]]).T

    random.seed(1)

    synaptic_weights = 2 * random.random((3, 1)) - 1

    for iteration in xrange(10000):

        output = 1 / (1 + exp(-(dot(training_set_inputs, synaptic_weights))))
```

```
        synaptic_weights +=
dot(training_set_inputs.T,
(training_set_outputs - output) * output * (1 -
output))

        print 1 / (1 + exp(-(dot(array([1, 0, 0]),
synaptic_weights))))
```

Questions

- What are the pros and cons of connecting layers to pass along information and perform a detailed analysis of the input being passed through?

- What is the process by which the average networks see images?

- What is the purpose of training data?

Neural Networks and Data Analytics

With the wide variety of complicated methods of statistical analysis that are available today, artificial neural networks can also be used for a wide variety of things including stock market analysis, speech or face recognition, fraud detection and even medical diagnostics. What's more, given the right variables, it can accurately predict future variables without directly dealing with the relationships that underlie the affect that certain variables have on one another. Alternatively, it can be used to accurately pinpoint relationships that otherwise might seem too complex to map accurately. In this case, the machine learning techniques that are being called into play actually successfully match patterns present in human cognition which means that it is learning from the past in order to predict the future.

The first time that the pattern is detected, the network will guess as to what the outcome is going to be, it then cycles and sees if its results were accurate, and if not, how inaccurate they actually were. Using the actual results as well as the estimated results, it then retries a new hypothesis and repeats the cycle as needed.

Due to the fact that the specifics of the space or margin of error is impossible to deduce ahead of time, it is common for analysis done via a neural network to take a significant number of tests, called runs, in order to come up with what is likely to be the most effective solution moving forward. This speed can be adjusted through what are known as mathematical assist terms. This helps for the network to build a steady momentum and reach a reliable answer more quickly.

After a neural network has reached a level where it has a clear idea of what is going on in regards to a given problem, it can then be given additional types of data to work with. This can be done by forcing the network to work in propagation mode moving forward. This will ensure that new inputs are factored through the lens of prior inputs and are not simply replacing them.

When pursuing this course of action, it is important to keep in mind that a neural network can be trained exhaustively regarding a certain type of input that it becomes unreliable when used with any other types of input. This is referred to as being grandmothered and is guaranteed to leave your neural network practically useless.

Multilayer Perceptron Neural Network

The multilayer perceptron model is a type of neural networking model that matches relevant inputs with related outputs. It is comprised of numerous layers of nodes set up so that its vertices are connected by the edges but each edge has a specific direction it is associated with as well. Each of these layers is then connected fully to the ones on either side of it. Additionally, while the input node is different, the remainder of the nodes can be thought of as neuron, or processing core, with a specific activation function, just like in a more traditional neural network. It is superior to the more common type of neural network as it is capable of more clearly distinguishing data that is not separable in a linear way.

It is this ability to consider activation functions that are nonlinear as well as the more common linear options that are available in a more traditional neural network. This allows it to determine the frequency of action potentials in much the same way that neurons fire in your own brain. This idea can be expressed through the activation function that can be written as $y(v_i)=\tanh(v_i)$ as well as $y(v_i)=1+e^{-v1})^{-1}$. In this case, y is going to be the output of the ith node while v_i can be thought of as the sum of the input after it has been appropriately weighted. There are other types of activation functions that can be used including radial basis function, softplus function and rectified functions.

The phrase multilayer perceptron can be confusing to some people because the model can be considered not as a single perceptron with many layers but instead a group of perceptron working in layers towards a group goal. What' s more, these groupings of perceptrons aren't even true perceptrons in the traditional sense as they aren't bound to a single activation function but are instead free to take that which makes the most sense in the moment.

Through the use of the same type of backpropagation algorithm that can be seen in a standard neural network, multilayer perceptrons can be found as part of the standard analysis algorithm for pattern recognition processes around the world, though they are especially useful when it comes to parallel distributed processing and computational neuroscience. They are also found in research where the data is particularly difficult to approximate successfully as is the case with things like approximating someone's overall level of fitness. Additionally, they are known to function as universal aproximators which means they are useful when it comes to creating models that are based on types of regression analysis. They can also be used as a type of classification for regression if the response is likely to be categorical.

Support Vector Machine

When it comes to machine learning, a support vector machine is a type of supervised learning model which uses a variety of algorithms associated with learning in an effort to analyze data for easier use with either regression analysis or classification. When a support vector machine is given a group of examples for the purpose of training, then each is marked as belonging to one of a pair of categories which, in turn, makes it easier to classify future objects into one of the categories. This makes it what is known as a binary linear classifier of the non-probalistic variety.

Once it is fully generated, a support vector machine model is a visual representation of numerous points in space but mapped in such a way that the categories that have been defined are clearly separated from one another via a gap that you will want to be as large as possible. From there, when new examples are added to the model it will generate a predication as to what side of the gap it is going to fall on.

What's more, support vector machines are known to be able to effectively classify in a non-linear way as well through the use of something known as feature space that is high dimensional. This means that a support vector machine can also be used effectively if the data you are working with has not previously been tested and labeled properly. In these instances, it can use what is known as an unsupervised learning approach which allows it to look at the way the data in question groups naturally before mapping additional data to these various groups as it is acquired. This ability is what is known as support vector clustering and is most commonly used in industrial settings where it can be difficult to ensure that data is labeled properly as it is generated.

Specifically, the support vector machines that you will be likely working with are constructed using at least one hyperplane that is located in a dimensional space that is infinite, or at least high. It can then be used for tasks like regression or classification as the separation between data will occur naturally and will be visible as the hyperplane that has the greatest amount of distance between itself and a local training data point or functional margin. Remember, the larger the margin is, the lower the overall classifier generalization error is going to be.

Naive Bayes Classifier

In machine learning it is important to be able to construct classifiers, more specifically, class labels that are assigned by models which are drawn from a predetermined list of classifiers. It is not just one algorithm but a variety of algorithms that share one thing in common. Specifically, they assume that the value of a feature is not related to the value of any other features related to that same variable. On the contrary, a naive Bayes classifier will consider each feature for what it contributes independently to the overall probability of the question in question without worry about correlations between the individual features.

While some probability model types can be naturally trained using naive Bayes classifiers via a supervised learning session, it will often be difficult in practice as the parameter estimation that is often used in models made using the naive Bayes method which focus on maximum likelihood of an event happening instead. While this type of classification and assumption may seem oversimplified, they traditionally prove quite successful in real world settings time and again. One of the reasons it remains so effective is that it requires relatively little in terms of training data before parameters of effect can begin to be estimated.

While the more far reaching of naive Bayes assumptions can prove inaccurate, there are several other properties that prove it is useful in many scenarios. Specifically, when it comes to decoupling class conditional distribution of features a naive Bayes can be used to properly determine the distribution element by simply estimated each as a dimensional distribution with only one dimension. Doing so can help prevent problems for occurring when it comes to more complicated types of dimensionality, specifically the need for sets of data to scale properly with the number of features that are currently being explored.

Despite the fact that a naive Bayes is often known to fail when it comes to producing accurate class probability estimates this is not actually a requirement for all applications which means it can still be extremely useful as long as you take its limitations into account. Instead, it is perfectly acceptable for the naive Bayes to instead make the appropriate decision based on classification of which classification is most likely, even if there are no other classification options available to it. This will also be true no matter if the probability is inaccurate, no matter if the degree to which it is inaccurate is vast or microscopic. As such, the overall classifier can still be soundly robust enough that it has the ability to shrug off major deficiencies related to the naive probability model that it underlines.

Questions

- How is the Multilayer Perceptron Neural Network different from other types of neural networks?

- In what scenario is the Multilayer Perceptron Neural Network most useful?

- What type of classifications are support vector machines capable of?

Common Mistakes to Avoid

Failing **to normalize data:** When working with neural networks, it is important to always keep in mind how your data is going to be normalized. This is an extremely vital step and if you miss it then you have little chance of your network working properly. Unfortunately, if you find yourself following an online deep learning tutorial then you may find that this step is skipped because it is so basic that it is assumed it will be done as needed.

Broadly speaking, in this sense normalization means to subtract the mean from your data and then divide your data by the standard deviation. Generally this will be done for each input individually as well as for each output feature but you can do it for groups of features as well, be careful when grouping things together, however, as some features will require special care to normalize properly.

The reason that this step is so crucial is that a majority of the neural network's pipeline will assume that both the input and output data are processed in this way which means that this assumption occurs virtually everywhere which means training algorithms assume its there in the first place. As a general rule, a neural network that is untrained will output values that are somewhere between -1 and 1. If you are anticipating values in any other ranges you will naturally have some issues as the amount of work that will need to be done by the system to break beyond those ranges will be intense, if it works at all. Normalized the data prevents this issue from popping up in the first place.

A good rule of thumb is that the scale of a feature in a neural network will ultimately govern its importance. If you have a feature in the output that has a scale that is larger than average then it will be more likely to generate an error that seems large when compared to other, similar, features. Likewise, larger scale features in the input will typically dominate the network and thus cause even larger changes further down the line. Because of this, it often isn't always enough to use an automatic normalization process like those found in many neural network libraries which will blindly subtract the mean before diving by the standard deviation for each feature.

For example, you may find that you have an input feature that has an extremely small range such as .001 – 0. You would then need to consider if the range is this small because it is largely irrelevant, which could mean that it is fine the way it is, or if it is the way it is because of the way it is being compared to other features. The same goes for any features that end up with a range extremely close to, or exactly, 0 as these will lead to additional instabilities if you mistakenly try to normalize them.

Always check the results: Watching the number of errors suddenly start to decrease while going through the training process is a big moment. Unfortunately, unless you are very good or very lucky there is likely to be something else, somewhere that is wrong with your code. This could be something as simple as unwarranted inference, or it could be a bug in the training code or even the data preprocessing. Unfortunately, just because the error rate starts to decrease doesn't necessarily mean that the network is learning anything useful.

To ensure that it learns the right things it is important to take the time to really look at the data and determine its validity. Generally, this will mean visualize the results in an effective way, which can be difficult if your data doesn't easily lend itself to pictures and the like.

Regardless, you will need to implement a regular sanity check to ensure that everything is coming out properly at each stage of preprocessing, during training and throughout the inference pipeline when compared to the original ground truth data.

The reason for this is that, unlike more traditional programming, when a machine learning system fails it does so silently. Unlike with a traditional program that is likely to throw up error codes when something goes awry, there are no such checks with a neural network so you will need to check your processes at every stage of the process to ensure that there are no bugs hiding out somewhere. Luckily, there are still plenty of different ways to determine if a network is working correctly. To start, you will need to consider what the reported training error actually means. To do so you will need to visualize the result of the network as it is applied to the data in the training set.

Essentially what you are looking for is the way in which your network compares to the core truth in practice. While you may watch the error rate drop all the way down to .01, it will all be for not if that .01 creates an unacceptable result, in practice. If you find that what you are testing works on the training set, then the next step is to check it on the validation step as well to ensure that it properly works even when confronted with data that it hasn't seen previously.

The best thing to do is to work to get used to visualizing things in this way from the beginning instead of waiting for issues to arise first. Likewise, it is important to ensure that you always have a full pipeline in place prior to the running any experiments and that you have sanity checks built in all the way to the end user. While time consuming, this is the only way to truly evaluate a number of potential different approaches all at once.

Forgetting to preprocess the data: The fact of the matter is that most types of data is tricky and, generally speaking, data for things we know are similar can be numerically represented in dramatically different ways. For example, if you are animating a 3D character and were representing data using 3D positions based on the character's hypothetical joints relative to the center of motion. If this is the case, then facing one direction rather than the other may have dramatically different numerical representation. As such, it is important to represent different types of data differently to ensure that similar motions produce similar representations. For example, in some local reference frame (such as relative to the character's center of mass) so that both motions we know are similar get a similar numerical representation.

The easiest way to get started is to consider exactly what the features you are working with represent so that you can decide if there is some type of simple transformation you can do on them in order to ensure that the data points that represent the things you know are always going to result in similar representation from a numerical standpoint. This can be done by digging down into the features that are being represented so you can ensure that the data points that represent things you know are always going to generate this type of representation. You will also want to consider the possibility of a local coordinate system that could be used to represent the data in question in hopes of making things more natural. Good choices here include things like improved color space or different formatting.

This is an important consideration to make due to the fact that neural networks make only a handful of basic assumptions about the data that they are using as an input, and one of these essential assumptions is that the space that contains the data is, more or less, continuous which means that, for the most part, a point between two different data points is going to be a mix of the two data points and that two data points that are close to one another are going to have some core similarities. As such, having any discontinuities in the space of your data when it comes to such things is going to make the early task of learning more difficult.

You can also think of data preprocessing as an attempt to reduce the potential for a combinatorial explosion based on data variations. As an example, if the neural network working in 3D animation as described above then learning unique but similar sets for every character, location and orientation will limit the overall capacity of the network and thus its total efficiency.

Conclusion

Given the perspective provided by this book, I hope that your deep understanding of the operational level of a neural network enables you to go beyond the confines of re-creation and into the realm of reinvention.

It is worth giving credit to the power existing neural nets provide. This book, for example, was written largely aided by machine learning and artificial intelligence. Many portions of this book were dictated to a computer using speech recognition. Grammar and word choice suggestions were offered from neural networks. Text to speech was used to get a read-back of the chapters to make adjustments to readability. Consider the prevalence and influence of network technology in your day-to-day life.

Before you go forth and begin building your own networks, make sure you are armed with the resources that will empower you to be the best in the field. The following are a few of the talents and abilities you may want to entrain.

Math

We have learned and experienced that a neural network is a mathematical function primarily involving matrix multiplication. In addition to this, we have backward propagation that involves the use of linear regression and solving derivatives. These are domains of advanced algebra and calculus. Activation functions, like the sigmoid function, can be better understood if you have ever taken statistics.

Every part of a neural network is mathematical. In order to impact a hands-on change to a network's functioning, you will need to know how each part work. Even if you only assimilate the concepts intuitively, you will have greater leverage over the technical aspects of your network. As deep networks, in particular, become increasingly complex, producing mathematical solutions becomes more of an artistic, intuitive matter.

Computer Science

If you are to be interacting and engineering your own network, you will almost definitely need to be up to speed on computer science. This entails understanding the binary nature of computers, the difference between and capabilities of CPU and GPUs, and most importantly, how to write in at least one computer code language.

As mentioned in this book, a language called Python is a common code in neural networks, but Swift, Java, GO, and other codes can be used as well. As the field progresses, it is likely that the need to know these coding languages to structure your network will become obsolete in favor of user interfaces that only require simple clicking and typing. However, in keeping with the tone and position of this book, it is always recommended to equip yourself with the tools needed to reshape the very nature of machine learning. The code is infinitely versatile. User interfaces, while in some cases very powerful and sophisticated, define and thereby limit the reaches of creativity.

Psychology

Neural networks are well known for being inspired by the neurons of the central nervous system in the human body. That being said, this book clearly emphasizes many of neural network's shortcomings and dissimilarities existing between neural networks and the human mind. It is common to find that network engineers may be adept at the other required skillsets required to work with these sophisticated tools while lacking the introspective ability to scrutinize the model against the inner workings of his own thoughts and learning.

Consequently, you should place a high priority on the study of psychological theories including behavior cognition, and learning. Explore within yourself the logic that underlies your problem-solving abilities. Existing neural networks are almost like a synthetic chunk of brain tissue. In order for artificial intelligence to reach realization, these systems will need to learn to identify and discern between entities and Geoffrey Hinton points out. Basically, current networks aren't even remotely aware. To date, the concept of 'self' and 'external world' exists entirely undefined to networks simulating intelligence. It's a huge contextual awareness issue, and frankly, it's remarkable that machine learning has come this far without being designed with this primal concept. This, in combination with the absence of 'subjective certainty,' a concept introduced by this book, has networks exhibiting far less intelligence than many wild animals. I can train and reinforce a dog to understand a variety of hand signals in far less time and technical effort than any current neural network. Again, I urge you to take the wheel and fill these gaps in existing machine learning technology. The answers are hidden in plain sight when we re-address the operation from a creative stance.

Abstract Reasoning

When working with neural networks, most of what you engage will be non-physical. This requires sub-intelligence in the area of abstract reasoning. Study.com defines abstract reasoning as: "Abstract reasoning refers to the ability to analyze information, detect patterns and relationships, and solve problems on a complex, intangible level. Abstract reasoning skills include: Being able to formulate theories about the nature of objects and ideas."

I think that definition adequately highlights how critical abstract reasoning is in relation to the topic. Interestingly enough, this sub-intelligence is one that you should be comfortable with in order to analyze and improve the performance of the network, pattern recognition, and problem-solving in an intangible level is a task in which present networks excel.

Information Systems

A background in information systems will assist network training engineers. Networks use large volumes of data to train on, which could be tricky to structure for someone lacking such a foundation. Sometimes data you receive will be raw. This can mean the data may not have proper labels for the intended purpose of our network. Maybe values need to be translated, reformatted, rearranged, or even filtered. Finding, understanding, and appropriating data for use in a neural network is a challenging task in itself.

Logistics

Moving goods or information through some organization or system could be defined as logistics. As you can guess, moving massive amounts of data around could be messy if not properly organized and coordinated. There are some neural networks that are spread across several computers due to their size. Basically, these are single neural networks partitioned across multiple machines. There are a limited number of places that the data overlap in these types of networks. The problem is like having an image of a flower that you want to print as a poster, so you print it across 4 sheets of paper and then combine the parts appropriately. The difference, of course, is we are doing this with data on a network. The other network processing components don't know what the rest of the network is thinking. Information is not duplicated across the machines. Only a narrow intersection of information is shared. Can you imagine wiring up this sort of neural network RAID?

Creativity

Finally, but the most important thing, is creativity. Many times this book will urge you to take a creative approach when initiating into the world of neural networks, machine learning, and artificial intelligence. So many currently working in the field make small improvements or sometimes none at all. There is little virtue in merely repeating the practice of those before you. Those that think we are nearly there, save a few final small tweaks, stunt the ascension to the ultimate goal of general artificial intelligence.

In this book, you have become familiar with the history that gave rise to the neural networks we see in the world today. You have learned that their thought process is more like scoring and sorting. This book has outlined their elemental parts, combined with how they can be arranged into a structure that can perform intelligence-based tasks. In this book, you have also been exposed to current and former models for network training. You'll have a reference point from which to start structuring your own networks. All of this, as promised, presented in a nonmathematical, jargon-free, simple word form, using relatable examples. As you've been reading, you have been able to get a picture of the nature and principles of neural network operations. This is distinctly a different perspective than approaches rooted in the mathematical and technical side of things. My hope is that this wisdom will enable you to easily build on the knowledge you received, while also empowering you to enact meaningful changes to the work.

Now that you know what a neural network is, you also know what it is not. You may have found that the way neural networks actually function did not match what you were expecting. To you, I say, use that gap in reality versus expectation as an indicator for what degree the overall concept has to improve. We have learned that they are not intuitive, rather, a math problem that can simulate learning through scoring probabilities. This is no way similar to how you classify the world around you. As Geoffrey Hinton once pointed out in a lecture, networks have no concept of entities. They make no distinction between self and environment.

You've also learned that neural networks require tons of training and training data, passed through thousands of times in order to achieve adequate training. This includes cases where training data is non-sophisticated, like the classification of handwritten numbers zero thru nine. Many believe the key to making strides with the technology is to improve the performance of the hardware that powers it. It should be apparent, however, that the structure is waiting to be reimagined entirely. Networked types should be as numerous and diverse as the companies that employed them. You can think of them as different species of creatures. There is no one way the process of machine learning and artificial intelligence should be put into practice. Always remember that machine learning and artificial intelligence can be achieved in an unlimited number of ways.

I hope that I've helped you in your mission of understanding neural networks and you enjoyed reading this book.

About the Author

Steven Cooper is a data scientist and worked as a software engineer at multiple startups. Now he works as a freelancer and helping big companies in their marketing and statistical analysis using machine learning and deep learning techniques.

Steven has many years of experience with coding in Python and has given several seminars on the practical applications of data science, machine learning, and deep learning over the years. In addition he delivers training and coaching services that help technical professionals advance their careers.

He loves to write and talk about data science, machine learning, and Python, and he is very motivated to help people developing data-driven solutions without necessarily requiring a machine learning background.

When not writing or programming, Steven enjoys spending time with his daughters or relaxing at the lake with his wife.

9 783903 331181